The End of the World

What Catholics Believe

GW00703504

E]

All booklets are published thanks to the
generous support of the members of the
Catholic Truth Society

CATHOLIC TRUTH SOCIETY

PUBLISHERS TO THE HOLY SEE

Contents

All rights reserved. First published 2014 by The Incorporated Catholic Truth Society, 40-46 Harleyford Road London SE11 5AY Tel: 020 7640 0042 Fax: 020 7640 0046. Copyright © 2014 The Incorporated Catholic Truth Society. Image, Page 7: The Four Horsemen of the Apocalypse by Albrecht Dürer © Burstein Collection/CORBIS.

ISBN 978 1 86082 907 9

Introduction

Fascination with the end of the world is almost as old as organised religion itself. Amongst every generation of Christians from the time of Christ to the present, influential movements within Christianity have believed that the return of Christ at the end of human history would occur within their own lifetimes. Even among those that conceded that the end of the world may not happen during the course of their own life span, there was still a need to determine a narrative of events concerning the last times. The disciples had questioned Jesus on this subject during the apocalyptic discourse on the Mount of Olives: "Tell us, when will this be, and what will be the sign of your coming and of the close of the age?" (*Mt* 24:3).

This curiosity about how the world will end is hardly surprising, however. Given that the Bible gives a fairly detailed account of events that will precede the last times, it is only natural that Christians would be inclined to reflect upon this wealth of material. An entire branch of theology known as 'eschatology' is devoted to the study of end-times literature. Taken from the Greek '*eschata*' (meaning 'last things'), the use of the word 'eschatology' was originally confined to the study of *de Novissimis* -

the four last things of death, judgement, heaven and hell (the final destiny of the individual); but it has since been expanded to include the study of the 'last things' of the universe, including the signs and events that are believed to precede the end of the world. Thus the word eschatology can be used to describe the end-time beliefs of any religion - such as Islamic, Jewish or Zoroastrian eschatology.

Today, one of the most prominent forms of Christian eschatology is the so-called 'rapture' theology taught by many Protestant evangelical preachers. Given the current widespread popularity of this material, and the relative paucity of equivalent, trustworthy Catholic books to provide an alternative, it is inevitable that many Catholics will find themselves being influenced by these teachings at some point in their lives. Yet the very basis of the rapture theology that currently dominates the shelves of religious book stores is actually based on dangerous ancient heresies which have long since been condemned by the Church. In addition to being led astray by the erroneous teachings of popular preachers, Catholics must also contend with dubious claims of unapproved private revelations and spurious prophecies which emanate from within Catholicism itself, and how to discern between these and the genuine apparitions and visions of saints and mystics.

Without arming ourselves with proper guidance, whilst being immersed in such ideas that are widely circulated in popular culture, the average Catholic can easily be led into serious error. The aim of this booklet is to provide just such guidance to negotiate our way through this veritable minefield of heresy. By examining the historical development of Catholic eschatology, we can see the true origin of many of these modern ideas, and discover exactly why they were so vigorously condemned by our saints and Church leaders in the first place.

Part One:
The Rise and Fall of the Millennium

The doctrine of the Second Coming of Christ is one of the most mysterious, yet also one of the most important teachings of the Christian faith. Also referred to as the 'Parousia' (from the Greek word 'presence'), mention of the Second Coming recurs throughout the New Testament. The idea that Christ would one day return to earth to execute God's judgement at the end of the world was first introduced by Jesus himself in the Gospels. Throughout his ministry, Christ had taught the disciples that he would soon be taken away from them, but promised that he would return again one day, coming with the clouds in glory as the apocalyptic Son of Man described in Dn 7:13-14. Indeed the term 'Son of Man' that Jesus frequently uses when referring to himself throughout the Gospels is deliberately intended to invoke this apocalyptic figure seen in the Book of Daniel.

Although we first find reference to the Second Coming of Jesus in the New Testament, many of the writings on this subject are based on certain Old Testament passages which describe God appearing in glory with his angels in order to bring judgement upon humanity:

Then the Lord will go forth and fight against those nations as when he fights on a day of battle. On that day his feet shall stand on the Mount of Olives which lies before Jerusalem on the east…Then the Lord your God will come, and all the holy ones with him. (*Zc* 14:3-4, 5)

This imagery of God descending upon the Mount of Olives on the Day of the Lord in the Book of Zechariah is intimately connected to the story of Christ's ascension into heaven upon this exact location, when the apostles were told by angelic messengers that Christ would return in the same manner they seen him depart:

So when they had come together, they asked him, "Lord, will you at this time restore the kingdom to Israel?" He said to them, "It is not for you to know times or seasons which the Father has fixed by his own authority. But you shall receive power when the Holy Spirit has come upon you; and you shall be my witnesses in Jerusalem and in all Judea and Samaria and to the end of the earth." And when he had said this, as they were looking on, he was lifted up, and a cloud took him out of their sight. And while they were gazing into heaven as he went, behold, two men stood by them in white robes, and said, "Men of Galilee, why do you stand looking into heaven? This Jesus, who was taken up from you into heaven, will come in the same way as you saw him go into heaven." (*Ac* 1:7-11)

The question the apostles posed to the Risen Christ concerning the timing of the establishment of the Messianic kingdom encapsulates the major misunderstandings that would subsequently arise in relation to the Second Coming. The exact nature of the kingdom of God and when it would be established would remain a source of confusion for the first few centuries of Christianity, leading to the development of a variety of heretical teachings that still find widespread circulation today.

In contemporary Judaism, it was expected that the Messiah would come to establish an earthly kingdom by defeating the enemies of Israel, and usher in an era of universal peace and harmony. The fact that Jesus did not establish such an earthly kingdom, and was instead persecuted and crucified under the auspices of the Jewish Sanhedrin, presented the early Christian movement with one of its greatest stumbling blocks (*1 Co* 1:23). Yet Jesus had taught that his kingdom was not of this world (*Jn* 18:36), and that although the kingdom of God would only be fully consummated in the future upon his return (*Mt* 6:10; *Rv* 21:1-4), it was already now present through the course of his own ministry, and could be identified with the Church itself (*Lk* 17:21).[1] Christ told the disciples that the kingdom of God would not be coming in a way that could be observed (*Lk* 17:20), and that it was Satan who is the ruler of this world (*Jn* 12:31; cf. *1 Jn* 5:19). By totally renouncing any aspirations towards earthly political power during his temptation in the desert, Jesus had demonstrated that the true locus of his kingly authority lay over heaven itself.

Despite the consistency of these teachings throughout the New Testament, many early Christians persisted in the belief that Jesus would soon return and establish the earthly Messianic realm expected in contemporary Jewish apocalypticism.

The End is Nigh?

From the earliest days of Christianity, there was a widespread expectation of an imminent return of Christ. Even though Jesus had warned that the time of his return was unknown to anyone, and that it would only come when it was least expected (*Mt* 24:36-44), there were still many among the first generation of Christians who believed that the Parousia would occur within their own lifetimes. Some of the early followers of Jesus interpreted certain words of Christ to suggest that his return would take place before the first generation of Christians had died. Those words include: "Truly I tell you, there are some standing here who will not taste death before they see the Son of Man coming in his kingdom" (*Mt* 16:28); "Truly I tell you, this generation will not pass away until all these things have taken place" (*Mt* 24:34) and "For this we declare to you by the word of the Lord, that we who are alive, who are left until the coming of the Lord, shall not precede those who have fallen asleep. (*1 Th* 4:15)

Upon a cursory reading, these words could certainly give the impression that the return of Christ was imminent. Many of the first Christians understood this teaching to mean that Jesus would soon return to establish an earthly Messianic reign like that expected by contemporary Jews. In his Second Letter to the Thessalonians, St Paul redressed certain members of the Christian community in Thessalonica, as some of their number had quit their daily work in order to prepare for the Second Coming of Christ.

In the nineteenth and twentieth centuries, some advocates of the historical-critical method used passages such as this to suggest that the writers of the New Testament mistakenly believed that Jesus would return during their lifetimes. Yet when we examine the eschatology of the New Testament in closer detail, it gives various details which would require a considerably long period of time to unfold between the apostolic age and the Second Coming of Christ. St Paul instructed the Christian community at Thessalonica not to become overly agitated in awaiting the Parousia, as there was a set series of events that would have to take place before the Second Coming. In particular, St Paul taught that there would be a major falling away of Christians before the return of Christ, in a time period which has subsequently been termed the Great Apostasy:

Now concerning the coming of our Lord Jesus Christ and our assembling to meet him, we beg you, brethren, not to be quickly shaken in mind or excited, either by spirit or by word, or by letter purporting to be from us, to the effect that the day of the Lord has come. Let no one deceive you in any way; for that day will not come, unless the rebellion comes first, and the man of lawlessness is revealed, the son of perdition. (*2 Th* 2:1-3)

Here, St Paul expanded upon the words of Jesus during his apocalyptic discourse on Mount Olivet, when he told the disciples that one of the signs that would precede his coming would be a general apostasy of Christians:

And then many will fall away, and betray one another, and hate one another. And many false prophets will arise and lead many astray. And because wickedness is multiplied, most men's love will grow cold. (*Mt* 24:10-12)

It was in contemplating this future event that prompted Christ's despairing words "when the Son of man comes, will he find faith on earth?" (*Lk* 18:8). The expectation of a general apostasy of Christians during the last days is cited by the *Catechism of the Catholic Church* as one of the events that must take place before the Parousia of Christ:

Before Christ's second coming the Church must pass through a final trial that will shake the faith of many believers. The persecution that accompanies her pilgrimage on earth will unveil the "mystery of iniquity" in the form of a religious deception offering men an apparent solution to their problems at the price of apostasy from the truth.[2]

Given the fact that Christianity was still very much a fledgling movement in a state of rapid expansion by the time the Second Letter to the Thessalonians was composed, St Paul clearly expected this mass apostasy to occur at some point in the distant future, well beyond the life-span of any living Christian. Christ had called upon the apostles to "make disciples of all nations" during the Great Commission (*Mt* 28:18-20), and had promised that the Gospel would be spread to all peoples before the end of the world (*Mt* 24:14). As the most ardent of all missionaries, St Paul would have been quite aware of his own limitations, and that the command to proclaim the Gospel to the ends of the earth would be unachievable during his own lifetime. Moreover, in his Letter to the Romans, St Paul had taught that the general resurrection of the dead would only take place once the Jews had finally accepted the Gospel (*Rm* 11:15), and that this would only happen once the "fullness of the gentiles" was brought in at the accomplishment of the proclamation of the Gospel to the ends of the earth (*Rm* 11:25). So it is obvious that the writers of the New Testament envisioned a considerably lengthy expanse of time to separate the first coming of Christ from the Second Advent.

The passages which appear to predict that end-times events would occur within the life times of the first generation of Christians have numerous explanations. During his apocalyptic discourse, in which he told his listeners "this generation will not pass away until all these things have taken place", Jesus had also prophesied the destruction of the Temple in Jerusalem (cf. *Lk* 21:20). It was this event in AD 70 which proved to indeed actually be witnessed by the original audience Jesus was addressing.

Christ's words that "there are some standing here who will not taste death before they see the Son of Man coming in his kingdom" can be explained in the fact that immediately afterwards, Peter, James and John witnessed the Transfiguration (*Mt* 17:1-13), when Jesus revealed himself to them his glorified form. But a parallel passage can also be found in Jn 21:22-23, when after St Peter had enquired about the fate of St John, the Beloved Disciple, Jesus answered:

> "If it is my will that he remain until I come, what is that to you? Follow me!" So the rumor spread in the community that this disciple would not die. Yet Jesus did not say to him that he would not die, but, "If it is my will that he remain until I come, what is that to you?"

The above promise that the Beloved Disciple would remain alive until Jesus returned is most likely connected with the appearance of Christ to St John at Patmos several decades later, when he commanded him to write the Apocalypse (*Rv* 1:19). So Jesus's statement concerning some of those present remaining alive to see him coming in his kingdom, may also allude to the visions seen by St John while he was composing the Book of Revelation.

Montanism vs Public Revelation

Even after the first generation of Christians had passed away, the belief that Jesus would soon return was still a widespread feature of apocalyptic beliefs in the early Church during the second century AD. One of the most prevalent prophetic movements during this time period was the 'New Prophecy', established by the recent convert Montanus, who claimed that the Holy Spirit spoke directly through him, and that the Heavenly Jerusalem described in the Book of Revelation would soon literally descend upon the mountains of Phrygia in Asia Minor. Montanism was a highly influential belief system in some quarters of the early Church, and even managed to attract the attention of luminaries such as the Church Father Tertullian. The fact that Montanus asserted to have a direct line of communication to heaven highlighted the most serious difficulty with prophetic movements as a whole, and the challenge that such claims presented not only to the authority of the established Church hierarchy, but also to the central role of sacred Scripture itself.

Iontanus claimed that since his words were directly inspired by the Holy Spirit, they were thus a continuation of Scripture. By purporting that divine revelation was a continuing process, Montanism threatened not only to obscure the importance of the ministry of the apostles, but to also eclipse the teachings of Christ himself. This two-pronged assault on both sacred tradition and Scripture threatened to undermine the central tenets of the Christian faith, and Montanism was thus condemned as a dangerous heresy. The problems posed by the rise of Montanism was one of the primary factors which would force the Church to define the Christian canon, and to distinguish public from private revelations. Divine (or public) revelation ended with the death of the last apostle, and was directly inspired by God. While the Church recognised that God still communicates to particular individuals through private revelations and mystical experiences, such means of interaction with the supernatural is vastly inferior to apostolic teachings and writings, and is constantly beset with untrustworthy subjective elements that are open to interpretation.[3]

Millenarianism

For the first few centuries of Christianity, there was a lingering confusion over the nature of the millennial reign of Christ described in Rv 20. The Book of Revelation describes a "thousand year" era during which Satan would be bound, and the saints would come to life to reign with Christ. After this time is over, we are told that Satan would be once again unleashed for "a little while", to deceive the inhabitants of the earth and gather them together for battle before the general resurrection of the dead and the Last Judgement. Many of the first Christians, including several Church Fathers, such as Sts Justin Martyr and Irenaeus, took the chronology of this portion of the Apocalypse quite literally. According to an interpretation of the Book of Revelation which was subsequently identified as the heresy of chiliasm (derived from the Greek '*chilia*', meaning 'thousand'), Jesus would establish a millennial reign during his Second Coming, upon which he would rule on earth with the resurrected saints and inaugurate an era of unprecedented peace and tranquillity, fulfilling the expectation of the Messianic kingdom taught in Jewish tradition. St Irenaeus even went as far as to speculate that this period would be a time of great abundance, when nature would produce copiously once creation had been restored to its original pristine condition before the Fall.[4] The chiliasts believed that Satan would be bound during this interim future period of triumph for the Church, after the defeat of the Antichrist and False Prophet, and that evil would cease to exist until Satan was released again at the end of the thousand years to incite the final revolt of Gog and Magog before the general resurrection of the dead (cf. *Rv* 20:7-10).

The idea that Christ could appear at any moment to establish a paradise on earth was cathartic for many Christians who were living during an age of persecution from the local Roman authorities. The belief that their period of suffering would soon be reversed through divine intervention and righteousness would eventually prevail, proved to be extremely attractive. Some Gnostics, such as Cerinthus in the second century, took this idea a step further, and held that the millennial kingdom of Christ would be a period of delights, when the saints would be rewarded with great feasting and banquets. But most early Christian millenarians were more reserved in their expectations, and the widespread popularity of chiliasm survived until well into the fourth century, when it was still being championed by writers such as Lactantius in his *Divine Institutes*.

Many chiliasts attached their belief in the millennium to the idea of a 'Great Week', wherein the age of the universe would span a week of millennia, in accordance with the days of creation described in the Book of Genesis. Following a line of logic derived from 2 P 3:8: "with the Lord one day is like a thousand years, and a thousand years are like one day", many early Christians believed that the millennium would be the seventh thousand-year period since creation, and that this time period would be a Sabbath day of rest before the Last Judgement. Just as God rested on the seventh day after creation, so too would the saints be granted a time of peace and tranquility on earth as part of a 'first resurrection' at the dawn of the seventh millennium. Chiliasts thus argued that there would be two bodily resurrections - the first being the resurrection of the saints mentioned in Rv 20:5, followed a thousand years later by the general resurrection of the dead.

The notion that the age of the universe would encompass seven thousand years is present in the writings of St Irenaeus, who taught that Christ would come to defeat the Antichrist at the end of the sixth millennium and establish an earthly millennial kingdom.[5] This idea of a 'Great Week' was partially based on Plato's concept of a Great Year, when the classical planets known to the ancients would return to their original positions after a complete cycle of the precession of the equinoxes.[6] The length of a complete axial cycle of the equinoxes was accurately calculated as taking place every 25,800 years by the Greek astronomer Hipparchus, and was viewed as the transition of one astrological age to the next, when the world would be periodically devastated by either flood or fire. The completion of a Great Year was thought to be marked by an alignment of all seven of the classical planets at the end of this axial precession. The Babylonian astrologer Berossus, for example, asserted that the earth would be inundated when the planets assembled in the constellation of Capricorn, and consigned to flames when they gathered in Cancer.[7]

By combining the notion of a Great Year with a week of millennia corresponding to the seven days of creation, chiliasts could thus use this Great Week to effectively date the time of the Second Coming of Christ - if only they could pinpoint the exact date of creation. Many Christians in the early Church were concerned with the prophetic significance of the date of creation, and various attempts were made to calculate the exact point at which the universe was created by using the chronologies and genealogies detailed in the Bible. Before the Anno Domini calendar was devised by the Scythian monk Dionysius Exiguus in the sixth century, many Christians adhered to Anno Mundi dating system, which was calculated from the date of creation. A major flaw in this technique lay in the fact that whichever version of the Bible used could yield enormously different results for establishing the date of creation, which varied by almost fifteen hundred years. Using the Hebrew Masoretic text of the Old Testament, Rabbi Jose ben Halafta (second century AD) had established that the year of creation could be dated to 3761 BC, which is closely in line with the version of the Anno Mundi calendar still used by Jews today. Most Christians in the early Church used the Greek Septuagint version of the Old Testament however, the chronology of which provided a much earlier date for the creation of the world, with slightly varying results. Writing in the second century, St Theophilus of Antioch had determined that the world was created at around the year 5529 BC, whilst Julius Africanus dated creation to 5500 BC. This earlier dating for the year of creation meant that the Sabbath millennium expected by chiliasts would begin around the year AD 500. In the third century, St Hippolytus also held to the 5500 BC date for the creation of the world, and proposed that after six thousand years had elapsed, Christ would come to establish his millennial reign on earth.[8] This placed the Second Coming as occurring at around the year AD 500, and many chiliasts were looking towards this date with eager anticipation.

Amillennialism - Apocalypse Now

Not all early Christians were millenarians, however. St Justin Martyr noted in the second century that many Christians did not accept the view that Christ would reign with the resurrected saints on earth for a thousand years after his Second Coming.[9] Origen held that the millennium was allegorical in nature, and was one of the fiercest opponents of chiliasm. After the conversion of the Roman Emperor Constantine to Christianity in the early fourth century, the newly formed ties between the Church and the secular government radically changed the apocalyptic self-image of Christianity. The fact that Christians were no longer under the constant threat of persecution, and were now very much in favour with the Roman government, meant there was not such a pressing need for the total societal transformation that would be wrought by the Second Coming of Christ. During a time of extreme persecution, it was almost impossible for early Christians to comprehend that Satan was already bound, and that the millennial reign of Christ was already present in the Church.

Given that Christianity had triumphed over the Roman Empire before the Parousia, the early Church theologians were now free to contemplate whether Satan had already been vanquished, and that the millennial reign of Christ was already underway in the present.

After the conversion of Constantine, Eusebius of Caesarea embarked on an aggressive campaign of refuting the advocates of chiliasm, and was followed later in this assault by St Jerome. Orthodoxy was increasingly beginning to question if the rather worldly implications of chiliasm were compatible with the central message of the Gospel.

Even though this early form of premillennialism was already in decline in the fourth century, it was St Augustine of Hippo who finally laid the legacy of this heresy to rest. While Augustine had originally adhered to the millenarian position shared by many of his contemporaries, he soon found the focus of chiliasm on the importance of the material world to be grossly deficient. Drawing on the earlier work of the influential Donatist writer Tyconius, St Augustine highlighted the fact that Jesus taught that Satan was already bound as a consequence of his own ministry, and had suffered his ultimate defeat through Christ's sacrificial death on the Cross. As such, the millennial reign of Christ was already well underway.

To support this argument, Augustine pointed out that the Apocalypse's description of Satan being chained for a "thousand years" in the abyss (*Rv* 20:1-3) was to be directly equated with the binding of the "strong man" in *Mt* 12:29: "…how can one enter a strong man's house and plunder his property, without first tying up the strong man? Then indeed the house can be plundered."[10] For St Augustine, the binding of Satan for a thousand years did not mean that evil would cease to exist throughout the course of the millennium (as was held by the chiliasts), but rather that the power of the Devil would be restrained so that he could not prevent the spread and acceptance of the Gospel. As such, the purpose of binding the Devil was so that Christ could plunder the possessions of the lord of this world through the proclamation of the Gospel. As Augustine puts it:

> '…the binding of the devil is his being prevented from the exercise of his whole power to seduce men, either by violently forcing or fraudulently deceiving them into taking part with him. If he were during so long a period permitted to assail the weakness of men, very many persons, such as God would not wish to expose to such temptation, would have their faith overthrown, or would be prevented from believing; and that this might not happen, he is bound.'[11]

This teaching is reflected in the *Catechism of the Catholic Church*, which also holds that although the ultimate defeat of Satan was won by the eternal sacrifice of Christ upon the Cross, this conquest over the Devil does not spare the Church from the continued existence of evil:

> Though already present in his Church, Christ's reign is nevertheless yet to be fulfilled "with power and great glory" by the King's return to earth. This reign is still under attack by the evil powers, even though they have been defeated definitively by Christ's Passover. (CCC 671)

> Before his Ascension Christ affirmed that the hour had not yet come for the glorious establishment of the messianic kingdom awaited by Israel which, according to the prophets, was to bring all men the definitive order of justice, love and peace. According to the Lord, the present time is the time of the Spirit and of witness, but also a time still marked by "distress" and the trial of evil which does not spare the Church and ushers in the struggles of the last days. It is a time of waiting and watching. (CCC 672)

St Augustine taught that the actual duration of the millennium could be interpreted in two ways. The first of the options he put forward was that it referred to a literal thousand years, and that this period should be calculated from the time of Christ. If correct, this thousand-year period would have ended around the year AD 1000. Augustine's second suggestion was that the millennium was symbolic in nature, and would last from the binding of Satan during the ministry of Christ, until near the end of the world at some undetermined point in the future, when Satan would be released for one final assault against the Church.[12] In this instance, a thousand years simply represented a very long period of time, and was not intended to be a precise measurement.

According to St Augustine's understanding of the millennium, the unbinding of Satan at the end of the thousand years is directly related to the Great Apostasy, when the love of many grows cold because iniquity abounds (*Mt* 24:12). Indeed, Augustine even goes as far as to praise those Christians with the strength to persevere in the faith during the future time when Satan is unbound:

> 'And what are we in comparison with those believers and saints who shall then exist, seeing that they shall be tested by the loosing of an enemy with whom we make war at the greatest peril even when he is bound?'[13]

Following this line of interpretation, the amillennialist position forwarded by St Augustine equates the unleashing of Satan at the end of the thousand years with the rise to power of the Antichrist, rather than the overly literal understanding of the chronology of the Apocalypse followed by the chiliasts. According to the chiliastic/

premilliennial interpretation of the Book of Revelation, there are two separate bodily resurrections: the resurrection of the just, which occurs at the beginning of the millennium during the Parousia; and the general resurrection of the dead which takes place once the thousand years are over. The Antichrist and False Prophet are thrown into the lake of fire during the Second Coming of Christ at the beginning of the thousand years, and the revolt of Gog and Magog at the end of the millennium is considered to be a separate event from the reign of the Antichrist. So not only do we have two separate resurrections in a chiliastic interpretation of the Apocalypse, but also two different periods during which Satan attacks the Church.

The amillennial approach outlined by St Augustine followed St Victorinus of Pettau's insight that the structure of the Apocalypse was recapitulatory in nature, which meant that there was no strict chronological order to be found within the Book of Revelation. For Augustine, the assault of Gog and Magog on the camp of the saints/Church at the end of the millennium, before their destruction by fire falling from heaven, was identical with Christ destroying the Antichrist with the breath of his mouth described in 2 Th 2:8.[14] This meant that the defeat of the Antichrist and False Prophet described in Rv 19:19-20 actually takes place once the millennium is over, rather than before it, as was suggested by the chiliasts. This sequence of events, which depicts just one final onslaught of Satan against the Church, is affirmed by the *Catechism* - which states not only that Christ *already reigns on earth* through the Church, but also that the triumph of Christ's kingdom can only take place after *one last assault* by the forces of Satan:

> Christ the Lord already reigns through the Church, but all the things of this world are not yet subjected to him. The triumph of Christ's kingdom will not come about without one last assault by the powers of evil. (CCC 680)

The triumph of God's kingdom occurs not during an interim, temporal period of finite duration, but only at the creation of the new heaven and new earth after the general resurrection and Last Judgement, when all things are put under the feet of Christ:

> Then comes the end, when he hands over the kingdom to God the Father, after he has destroyed every ruler and every authority and power. For he must reign until he has put all his enemies under his feet. The last enemy to be destroyed is death. For "God has put all things in subjection under his feet." (*1 Co* 15:24-27)

For St Augustine, there was only one bodily resurrection, and the 'first resurrection' mentioned in Rv 20:5 - when the saints come to life and reign with Christ for 'a thousand years', actually referred to the immediate resurrection of the soul after death.[15] As the Catechism teaches, the saints already reign with Christ, and will do so forever:

> "In the glory of heaven the blessed continue joyfully to fulfill God's will in relation to other men and to all creation. Already they reign with Christ; with him "they shall reign for ever and ever." (CCC 1029)

The 'first resurrection' of the saints is that which was won through the death and resurrection of Christ, when Jesus opened up the gates of heaven through his sacrifice on the Cross. Pope Benedict XII formally defined the reality of the immediate resurrection of the soul in his 1336 Apostolic Constitution *Benedictus Deus*, which is cited by the *Catechism*:

> "the souls of all the saints... and other faithful who died after receiving Christ's holy Baptism (provided they were not in need of purification when they died, … or, if they then did need or will need some purification, when they have been purified after death, ...) already before they take up their bodies again and before the general judgement - and this since the Ascension of our Lord and Savior Jesus Christ into heaven - have been, are and will be in heaven, in the heavenly Kingdom and celestial paradise with Christ, joined to the company of the holy angels." (CCC 1023)

After Christ granted the faithful departed entrance into heaven through his death and resurrection, the immortal soul would immediately face a 'particular judgement' once it is separated from the body upon death:

> Each man receives his eternal retribution in his immortal soul at the very moment of his death, in a particular judgement that refers his life to Christ: either entrance into the blessedness of heaven - through a purification or immediately, or immediate and everlasting damnation. (CCC 1022)

It was this immediate resurrection of the soul after death that St Augustine equated with the 'first resurrection' of Rv 20:5, and took pains to differentiate this event from the reunification of the body and soul during the general resurrection of the dead at the end of time. The amillennialist position advanced by St Augustine was of enormous influence within the Church, and shaped the development of all future Catholic theology relating to the end times. Amillennialism remained the unchallenged approach to interpreting the Apocalypse within Christianity until the Middle Ages, and this Augustinian tradition is still the authoritative view in contemporary Catholic eschatology.

Part Two: The Influence of Private Revelations on Catholic Apocalypticism

The Last World Emperor

Over the centuries, certain traditions concerning the end times were developed independently of Scripture, which mostly originated through apocalyptic speculation and the influence of various private revelations. One of the earliest such scripturally independent eschatological traditions was the idea of a Great Monarch, who it was foretold would arrive to rescue the Church from a state of desolation just before the coming of the Antichrist.

The earliest prophecy of the appearance of a Great Monarch who would establish an era of peace and bring about mass conversions before the age of the Antichrist is found in the Latin version of the Tiburtine Sibyl. *The Sibylline Oracles* were a collection of prophecies of various origin attributed to pagan prophetesses, but in reality were mostly composed by Jewish and Christian writers between the second and sixth centuries. As such, the original source of this prophecy is rather questionable in nature. This does not necessarily preclude the authenticity of the original source of the Great Monarch prophecies, however, since the Catholic Church recognises that God can speak through anyone, whether they are good or evil.[16] We need only to look to the wicked Baalam's famous Messianic "star prophecy" (*Nb* 24:17), or the High Priest Caiaphas's prophetic insight that Jesus must die for the sake of the nation (*Jn* 11:50-52) to find scriptural evidence that even evil people are capable of genuine prophecy. St Thomas Aquinas famously defended the prophetic authenticity of *The Sibylline Oracles*, and concluded that:

> The prophets of the demons do not always speak from the demons' revelation, but sometimes by Divine inspiration. This was evidently the case with Balaam, of whom we read that the Lord spoke to him (*Nb* 22:12), though he was a prophet of the demons, because God makes use even of the wicked for the profit of the good. Hence He foretells certain truths even by the demons' prophets, both that the truth may be rendered more credible, since even its foes bear witness to it, and also in order that men, by believing such men, may be more easily led on to truth. Wherefore also the Sibyls foretold many true things about Christ.[17]

The fact that the Church teaches that anyone is capable of genuine prophecy leaves the problem of knowing which prophecies to accept as authentic, and which to dismiss as deception of human or demonic origin. The Catholic Church adopts a very cautious attitude towards private revelations, and has accredited only a select few as "worthy of belief". In order to do so, the Church must first establish that the source of any such private revelation is definitely of supernatural origin, and cannot be attributed to being the product of human trickery or preternatural causes. The process of Church approval therefore normally requires a lengthy period of investigation by Church authorities, who are tasked not only to find proof of miraculous involvement, but also that any such private revelation contains nothing contrary to the faith or morals.

The fact that prophecies concerning the Great Monarch have been attributed to canonised saints, and that reference to this figure is included among the words of at least one Church-approved Marian apparition, makes these private revelations worthy of serious consideration.[18] But given that many differing and often conflicting variants of this prophecy began to circulate since medieval times, it is best to view it in the context of its historical development. The Tiburtine Sibyl explicitly based its concept of this eschatological restorer figure on the example of the Roman Emperor Constantine, who almost single-handedly brought about the conversion of the Empire to Christianity. Whilst millenarianism was in rapid decline in the wake of St Augustine, the idea that the world would be renewed through the influence of an earthly political figure became immensely popular. Rather than the chiliastic notion of Christ coming to restore the earth for a thousand years after the Parousia, the hope that the world could be renewed through the intervention of an earthly ruler before the coming of the Antichrist helped to fill the void left in the absence of millenarianism.

References to the Great Monarch were made in various other influential works, such as a seventh century text known by scholars as the *Apocalypse of Pseudo-Methodius* (which was falsely attributed to the fourth century Church Father, St Methodius of Olympus). One of the most widely popularised notions concerning the Great Monarch is that it foretells the future restoration of the French monarchy. We can trace the origins of the connection between the Great Catholic Monarch and the French monarchy to the tenth century abbot, Adso of Montier-en-Der. In an apocalyptic text addressed to Gerberga, the sister of Otto I of Germany and future Queen of the Franks, Adso linked the already well-known prophecy of the Great Monarch with the example of the Carolingian Emperor Charlemagne, who founded the Holy Roman Empire at the beginning of the ninth century:

> Some of our learned men say that one of the Kings of the Franks will possess anew the Roman Empire. He will be in the last time and will be the greatest and the last of all kings. After he has successfully governed his empire, he will finally come to Jerusalem and will lay aside his sceptre and crown on the Mount of Olives. This will be the end and the consummation of the Roman and Christian Empire.[19]

Adso had clearly viewed the life of Charlemagne as a precursor to the Great Monarch, and believed that history would recapitulate itself in the eventual fulfillment of this prophecy. For Adso, the establishment of the Holy Roman Empire in the relatively recent past was directly related to the *katechon*, or 'restraining force' which holds back the appearance of the Antichrist described in 2 Th 2:6.

Following the early Church Father Tertullian, the traditional exegesis of 2 Th 2 had previously equated this restraining force with the Roman Empire, which had been identified as the last of four apocalyptic beasts described in the Book of Daniel. Writing in the third century AD, Tertullian argued that the disintegration of the Roman Empire into ten separate kingdoms (relating to the ten horns of the beast described in *Dn* 7:7 and *Rv* 13:1) would precede the coming of the Antichrist.[20] When the final collapse of the Western Roman Empire in 476 failed to bring about the appearance of the Antichrist, there was a need to revise this interpretation. But the prevalence of the Roman Empire in relation to this prophecy was not quickly forgotten. In the Christian East, Byzantium, as the surviving eastern half of the ancient Roman Empire, was viewed as the natural continuation of the 'restraining force' which would hold back the coming of the Antichrist.

The idea of Byzantium being the restraining force prophesied in the writings of St Paul proved too geographically remote to resonate with the apocalyptic imagination of the Christian West. It took Charlemagne to unite Western Europe under the banner of the Holy Roman Empire in 800, before the identification of Rome as the restraining force of 2 Th found a renewed relevance in Western apocalyptic speculation. The writings of Adso, which made a connection between the prophecies of the future Great Monarch and the newly established Holy Roman Empire, helped to once again solidify the importance of Rome for interpreting the meaning of the biblical *katechon* in the Western apocalyptic tradition, and the Last World Emperor himself came to be associated with the restraining force of 2 Th 2. It was only in later history, when the term 'King of the Franks' became more distanced from the Holy Roman Empire established by the Frankish emperor Charlemagne, that the figure of the Great Monarch became more closely attached to the French monarchy in particular. The original and arguably most authentic prophecies are not quite so specific in scope, however.

The Joachite Movement and the 'Papal Antichrist'

The legend of the Last World Emperor was one of many later, non-biblical innovations to be introduced into the arena of Catholic Apocalypticism. During the Middle Ages, the idea of several other unique end-time figures and scenarios emerged, fuelled by the spread of apocalyptic speculation combined with the continual unfolding of private revelations. The single most influential apocalyptic author of this time period was undoubtedly the Calabrian abbot Bl. Joachim de Fiore (1135-1202), whose work led to the re-emergence of millenarianism in non-mainstream medieval eschatology.

As a whole, the Catholic Church had by now well settled into the Augustinian tradition that history would continue to progress in a spiritual equilibrium until the unbinding of Satan at the end of the 'millennium' (or age of the Church). This would then culminate in the appearance of the Antichrist during the age of the Great Apostasy - who would ultimately be destroyed by Christ during his Second Advent, before the destruction of the world by fire and the creation of the new heaven and the new earth.

Joachim de Fiore rejected this view, and envisaged the coming of a prolonged Golden Age for Christianity on earth after the defeat of the Antichrist. For the Calabrian abbot, the whole of human history was modelled on the Holy Trinity, and would be divided into three different *status* (ages) corresponding to this inherent trinitarian nature. The first *status*, which encompassed the period of the Old Testament, was the age of the Father. The second age began with the coming of the Son and continued into the present age of the Church. For Joachim, the third *status*, which was still to come, would belong to the Holy Spirit, and would usher in an era that would see the dissolution of the Church hierarchy. During this imminent new age of the Holy Spirit, humanity would be enlightened by the gift of the Paraclete, and Scripture would finally be understood in its totality. After the arrival of the *status* of the Holy Spirit, which Joachim believed would appear by the year 1260 (based on an interpretation of the 1,260 days of Rv 11) the necessity for a Church hierarchy would be rendered obsolete, and instead, the Church would be presided over by a new type of monastic movement referred to as the Order of the Just.

The Calabrian abbot equated the third *status* with the millennium of Rv 20 (although he did not consider this to be a literal thousand-year period), and warned that the dawn of this new age would not begin until the defeat of the Antichrist, who he thought was already in the world. Joachim posited that there would be two Antichrists, one at the dawn of the third *status*, and one at the end - *magnus Antichristus* (great Antichrist), whose arrival was imminent, and *ultimus Antichristus* (final Antichrist).[21] This view was seemingly necessitated by the appearance of the forces of Gog at the end of the millennium in Rv 20:8. It was believed that the Antichrist would ape the ministry of Christ to the extent that he also would have two separate historical manifestations, with the *ultimus Antichristus* being equated with the rise of Gog at the end of the third *status*.

For Joachim, there were also two different aspects of the *magnus Antichristus* to be found in the symbolism of the beast from the sea and the beast from land (*Rv* 13): that

of the roles of priest and king. Just as Christ was both king
and priest following the order of Melchizedek (*Heb* 7), so
too would the Antichrist assume the role of both king and
priest by usurping the papacy itself:

> Just as the Beast from the Sea is held to be a great king
> from his sect who is like Nero and almost emperor of
> the whole world, so the Beast ascending from the earth
> is held to be a great prelate [*magnum prelatum*] who
> will be like Simon Magus and like a universal pope
> [*universalis pontifex*] in the entire world. He is that
> Antichrist of whom Paul said he would be lifted up and
> opposed to everything that is said to be God, or that
> is worshipped, and that he would sit in God's temple
> showing himself as God [*2 Th.* 2:4].[22]

It is here that we find the kernel of the extremely
dangerous idea of a papal Antichrist-type figure, which
would later be exploited to its fullest extent during the
Reformation. Although Joachim de Fiore's theories were
condemned as heretical by Pope Alexander IV in 1263, his
work continued to be vastly influential in the development
of medieval apocalypticism, and would coalesce into a
wider movement known as the Joachism.[23] The Joachites
first emerged from certain factions within the Franciscan
Order, and were even more radical than Joachim de Fiore,
in that they attempted to apply some of his ideas as a means
of attack against the contemporary papacy.

The Franciscans had been divided over the extent to which the rule of St Francis concerning the vow of poverty should be implemented, and were divided into two camps - the Spirituals, who taught an extreme form of poverty, and the more moderate Conventuals. The ideals espoused by the Spiritual Franciscans were frowned upon by several popes, and the level of antagonism that existed between this radical movement and the papacy soon found its way into the prophetic literature of the Spirituals. A key figure among the Franciscan Spirituals, Peter Olivi (1248-1298), developed upon Joachim de Fiore's ideas concerning the dual 'priest-king' aspect of the Antichrist, and proposed that the sea-beast and land-beast of Rv 13 reflected the two-fold nature of the final enemy, which was comprised of the Mystical Antichrist (*Antichristus mysticus*) and the Great Antichrist (*Antichristus magnus*). Olivi speculated that a false pope would be installed by a secular ruler, becoming the Mystical Antichrist who precedes the coming of the Great Antichrist.[24]

The Franciscan Spirituals were eventually condemned as heretical by Pope John XXII in 1317, but their ideas concerning the coming of a false pope had by now already become entrenched, and would frequently resurface in the propaganda of subsequent opponents of the papacy. The notion of a papal Antichrist figure was not only one of the major driving forces in the thought of the Protestant Reformers, it still arises today - most notably among some circles of traditionalist Catholics. Many traditionalists fear that the Vatican hierarchy has become increasingly infiltrated by the forces of Freemasonry, which they believe seeks to destroy the Church from within by dismantling not only the liturgy itself, but also by abolishing core principles (such as Catholic teachings ranging from the doctrine of transubstantiation, to the Church's current position on topics such as marriage, contraception, abortion and homosexuality). A recurring theme among traditionalist Catholics is that Freemasonry has been working to achieve this goal by placing its own choice of papal candidate on the throne of St Peter, bringing to fulfilment not only Daniel's prophecy of the abomination of desolation, but also St Paul's warning about the 'Man of Sin' taking his place in the Temple of God (*2 Th* 2:3-4).

The election of Pope Francis has proven to be the latest concern to such groups, and a prophecy falsely attributed to St Francis of Assisi has been widely circulated, which apparently foretells the coming of a uncanonically elected 'destroyer pope', who will seek to destroy the Church from within. The provenance of this prophecy is not to be found among the authentic writings of the Seraphic Father, however, and almost certainly originated from the heretical Franciscan Spirituals. This bogus prophecy was lifted from a compilation of various writings attributed to St Francis collected together by the Irish Franciscan friar Luke Wadding (1588-1657). Composed around 1650, at a time when scholarly precedent was less stringent in regards to citing original source material, Wadding's work contains many spurious works drawn from second-hand sources, such as another equally unreliable compilation by fellow Franciscan Mark of Lisbon (d. 1591).

Besides sowing the seeds of schism by undermining the role of the successor of St Peter, the proponents of such prophecies fail to take into account the fact that part of the promise by Christ when he founded the Church upon the rock of St Peter, was that the gates of hell would never prevail against it: "And I tell you, you are Peter, and on this rock I will build my church, and the gates of Hades will not prevail against it." (*Mt* 16:18) Moreover, a central tenet of the Catholic faith is that the Holy Spirit nurtures and guides the Church to the truth throughout the whole of human history, making it impossible for the united Body of Christ under the Sacred Magisterium to err in matters of doctrine. The infallibility of the Church especially pertains to the office of the Bishop of Rome, who "enjoys, by reason of the Divine assistance promised to him in blessed Peter, that infallibility with which the Divine Redeemer wished His Church to be endowed in defining doctrine regarding faith and morals".[25] As such, even if a truly wicked person was (for some unfathomable reason) validly elected by a papal conclave, it would be utterly impossible for him to change the infallible teachings of the Sacred Magisterium.

Even the original authors of the 'papal Antichrist' prophecies accepted this reality, and instead proposed that the *Antichristus mysticus* would be a *false* pope (i.e. an anti-pope), against which the true pope would stand opposed. A false rival claimant to the papacy simply cannot exist without the presence of a validly elected Roman pontiff. And since a validly elected pope cannot err on matters of faith and morals when speaking *ex cathedra,* nor change the infallible treasury of the Sacred Magisterium, it is impossible (and even futile) for the False Prophet or the Antichrist to inhabit such a role.

The Wheat and the Chaff
- Distinguishing Between True and False Prophecy

The ubiquity of spurious prophecies in existence during the Middle Ages can make distinguishing such false prophecies from authentic private revelations very difficult indeed. Upon even a cursory overview of the later 'prophecies' concerning the Great Monarch, it soon becomes evident that many of them contradict each other. For example, some prophecies claim that the Last Emperor will be German, not French in origin; and several differing names have been attached to the Great Monarch. These inconsistencies inform us that we are dealing with apocalyptic speculation in many instances here, rather than genuine private revelations. In addition, there are a large number of prophecies concerning the

Great Monarch that claim to emanate from saints who lived long before the legend of the Last World Emperor began to develop, rendering them as demonstrably false. As noted above, historians have accurately traced the origin of these prophecies back to the Tiburtine Sibyl and Pseudo-Methodius somewhere between the fourth and seventh centuries. Yet in some of the most widely known compilations dealing with this subject, such as *Catholic Prophecy*, by Yves Dupont and *Trial, Tribulation and Triumph*, by Desmond Birch, Great Monarch prophecies have even been attributed to some of the early Church Fathers, such as St Hippolytus, or St Augustine of Hippo - who lived many years before the earliest known historical references to the figure of the Last World Emperor.[26]

During the Middle Ages, compilations of prophetic texts became highly popular. Rather than having to scour through the original primary source material of various saints and mystics, books such as the *Mirabilis Liber* compiled many popular references to end-time prophecies together in one single volume. But in straying from the original sources in a miscellany of prophetic texts, it became commonplace for the imprudent researcher to insert spurious prophecies of uncertain origin into such compilations. These prophetic compilations facilitated a number of bogus prophecies to achieve a wide circulation, and gradually, they became accepted as authentic by their general audience. Given that mention of such prophecies was repeated in other similar works, with no concern in finding their original sources, scholarly precedent in prophetic compilations was widely ignored. It was common to ascribe such prophecies to a person of renown in order to lend a greater air of credibility, and we find that some of these spurious end-time predictions have been attributed to saints who were widely known to have received apocalyptic visions. This set of circumstances makes it extremely difficult for the lay reader to distinguish such spurious works from the genuine writings of famous saints.

The German abbess St Hildegard of Bingen (1098-1179), for example, was widely revered during her own lifetime, and was accorded the title 'Sibyl of the Rhine' due to the fame of her visionary writings. St Hildegard was a prolific writer, and issued a vast collection of material throughout her career, including three large volumes dealing with visionary theology, as well a significant body of personal correspondence. Rather unfortunately, certain unscrupulous individuals aimed to capitalise on this popularity, and mostly for reasons of propaganda, disseminated a number of false prophecies under the guise of her good name. One early example of such pseudo-Hildegardian literature was the anti-mendicant prophecy *Insurgent gentes,* which was widely circulated in the mid-thirteenth century. Another more recent prophecy attributed to St Hildegard, of uncertain date and origin, speaks of the appearance of a comet and the flooding of a great nation in the sea, and somewhat ironically, this is the most widely circulated prophecy attributed to St Hildegard of Bingen found on the internet.

The genuine prophetic visions recorded by St Hildegard, who was declared a Doctor of the Church by Pope Benedict XVI on 7th October 2012, are far more interesting, however. One of the most enduring and provocative visions documented by St Hildegard in her work *Scivias*, is her depiction of the assault and rape of the virgin Church by the Devil towards the end of five epochs symbolised by a series of apocalyptic creatures, an event which ultimately results in the birth of the Antichrist.[27] St Hildegard takes up this theme elsewhere, and explicitly states that the evil that besets the marred countenance of the virgin Ecclesia stems from within the Church itself - from the very priesthood tasked as her protector:

'…her face was stained with dust, her robe was ripped down the right side, her cloak had lost its sheen of beauty and her shoes had been blackened. And she herself, in a voice loud with sorrow, was calling to the heights of heaven, saying, "Hear, heaven, how my face is sullied; mourn, earth, that my robe is torn; tremble, abyss, because my shoes are blackened!...

"For my Bridegroom's wounds remain fresh and open as long as the wounds of men's sins continue to gape. And Christ's wounds remain open because of the sins of priests. They tear my robe, since they are violators of the Law, the Gospel and their own priesthood; they darken my cloak by neglecting, in every way, the precepts which they are meant to uphold; my shoes too are blackened, since priests do not keep to the straight paths of justice, which are hard and rugged, or set good examples to those beneath them. Nevertheless, in some of them I find the splendour of truth."[28]

Pope Benedict XVI reflected upon this recurring theme in the visions of St Hildegard on several occasions, and intimated that this prophecy is analogous in many ways to the modern child sexual abuse crisis.[29] Yet in each of her visions concerning the despoiling of the Church by Satan at the end time (which is synonymous with the "Great Apostasy" foretold in the New Testament), St Hildegard is careful to stress that the Church is destined to be transformed from this disfigured state in a period of glorious renewal:

Behold, the feet of the aforementioned female image appeared to be white, giving out a brightness above that of the sun. I heard a voice from heaven saying to me: "Even though all things on earth are tending toward their end, so hardships and calamities is bowed down to its End, nevertheless, the Spouse of my Son, though much weakened in her children, will never be destroyed either by the heralds of the Son of Perdition or by the Destroyer himself, however much she will be attacked by them. At the End of time she will arise more powerful and more secure; she will appear more beautiful and shining so that she may go forth in this way more sweetly and more agreeably to the embraces of her Beloved."[30]

The fact that the authentic visions of St Hildegard have been sidelined in sensationalist compilations to vastly inferior spurious prophecies masquerading under her name is a gross injustice, and only serves to obscure the profound spiritual depth of her genuine writings.

The widespread prevalence of such spurious prophecies prompts us to be extra vigilant when researching modern apocalyptic literature, as in doing so, we will often find ourselves confronted with specious material that draws us further away from the truth, instead of closer to it.

The Age of Mary

The best way to avoid confusion when studying private revelations of an apocalyptic nature is to limit our credence to the heavenly apparitions which have been approved by the Church, and treat everything that lies outside these bounds with a healthy dose of scepticism.

Before granting approval, the relevant Church authorities subject claims of apparitions to considerable scrutiny to determine their supernatural character, which includes not only examining the scientific evidence, but also analysing any accompanying messages to confirm that they are free from any doctrinal errors. So when approval has been granted, we know that the claims behind any of the alleged events have a high degree of trustworthiness. Since the dawn of the modern era, there have been a number of Church approved private revelations that carry such authority.

After St Margaret Mary Alacoque first established devotion to the Sacred Heart of Jesus at Paray-le-Monial in 1673, the Church entered an age of unprecedented major Marian apparitions. Beginning with a series of visions given to St Catherine Labouré in 1830, in which she was shown the Miraculous Medal, the Virgin Mary has appeared on several occasions to the most humble and unassuming of people (frequently children), either to convey apocalyptic messages directly, or to communicate implicitly through the symbolism of their timing and circumstance.

Writing at the beginning of the eighteenth century, before the age of major Marian apparitions even began, St Louis de Montfort demonstrated an extraordinary level of prescience concerning the role the Virgin Mary would play in the approach of the Second Coming of Christ:

'If...as is certain, the knowledge and the kingdom of Jesus Christ must come into the world, it can only be as a necessary consequence of the knowledge and reign of Mary. She who first gave him to the world will establish his kingdom in the world...

The salvation of the world began through Mary and through her it must be accomplished. Mary scarcely appeared in the first coming of Jesus Christ so that men, as yet insufficiently instructed and enlightened concerning the person of her Son, might not wander from the truth by becoming too strongly attached to her... But in the second coming of Jesus Christ, Mary must be known and openly revealed by the Holy Spirit so that Jesus may be known, loved and served through her. The reasons which moved the Holy Spirit to hide his spouse during her life and to reveal but very little of her since the first preaching of the gospel exist no longer...

In these latter times Mary must shine forth more than ever in mercy, power and grace; in mercy, to bring back and welcome lovingly the poor sinners and wanderers who are to be converted and return to the Catholic Church.'[31]

This present Marian age has witnessed the some of the most remarkable apparitions in Church history. The then Vatican Secretary of State, Cardinal Bertone, has listed the Marian phenomena which have the approval of the local diocesan bishops as those of St Maria Alphonse Ratisbonne in Rome, 1842; Our Lady of La Salette, in 1846; Our Lady of Mercy, when an image of the *Mater Misericordiae* moved its eyes for several days in Rimini,

Italy, 1850; Our Lady of Lourdes, in 1858; Our Lady of Hope, Pontmain, France, 1871; Our Lady of Gietrzwald, Poland, 1877; Quito, Ecuador, 1906, when an image of Our Lady of Good Success moved its eyes over twenty times; Our Lady of Fatima, 1917; Our Lady of Beauring Belgium, 1932-1933; Our Lady of Banneaux, Belgium, 1933; Siracusa, Italy, 1953, when an image of the Immaculate Heart of Mary wept for four days; Our Lady of Light, Zeitoun, Egypt, 1968 when hundreds of thousands witnessed an apparition of the Virgin Mary on the dome of a Coptic Church in Cairo, Egypt; Our Lady of Akita, Japan, 1973; and Our Lady of Kibeho, Rwanda, 1981-1989.[32] Since the publication of Cardinal Bertone's book in 2007, the apparitions of Our Lady of Laus to Benôite Rencurel between the years 1664-1718 were approved by Bishop Jean-Michel di Falco of Gap in 2008. This was followed in 2010, when Bishop David Ricken of Green Bay, Wisconsin, formally approved the apparitions of Our Lady of Good Help to Adele Brise in 1859.

According to St Louis de Montfort, the ever increasing role the Blessed Virgin Mary would play in the latter times would bring about the fulfillment of the Protoevangelium of Gn 3:14, when the head of the Serpent of Eden would finally be crushed through her motherly intervention. It is this great spiritual battle of the last days between the Church and the forces of Satan, symbolised by the War in Heaven described in Rv 12. The narrative of the Woman

Adorned with the Sun (who represents both the Virgin Mary and the Church) is an apocalyptic expansion of the Protoevangelium, and dramatises the final defeat of Satan, when the head of the Ancient Serpent is crushed by the Mother of God. This ultimate victory of the Church over the forces of evil has been closely identified with the Triumph of the Immaculate Heart of Mary, which accomplishes the inauguration of the era of peace promised by Our Lady of Fatima.

Although the idea of an era of peace is mostly associated with the apparitions of the Virgin Mary to the shepherd children of Fatima (which is widely regarded as the zenith of the modern Marian age), the expectation of an eschatological restoration of the Church after a period of apostasy is firmly rooted in Scripture. St Bonaventure equated this period of renewal with the descent of the Heavenly Jerusalem described in Rv 21:2-3, combined with the symbolic building of Ezekiel's Temple - from which water would flow to refresh the barren Dead Sea (*Ez* 47):

> Then the prophecy of Ezekiel will be fulfilled when the city comes down from heaven (*Ezk* 40); not indeed that city which is above, but that city which is below, the Church Militant which will then be conformed to the Church Triumphant as far as possible in this life. Then will be the building and restoration of the city as it was in the beginning. Then there will be peace. God alone knows how long that peace shall last.[33]

The renewal of the Church during the last days is equated with the eschatological outpouring of the Holy Spirit detailed in Jl 2:28-29, when the eternal Gospel is proclaimed to the ends of the earth (*Mt* 24:14). This period marks the beginning of the new Pentecost, and is related to the ministry of the Two Witnesses of Rv 11, when God sends the prophet Elijah to "turn the hearts of fathers to their children and the hearts of children to their fathers" (*Ml* 4:5-6).

Although the Two Witnesses are traditionally associated with two prophets who ascended into heaven (Elijah and Enoch), we should not limit the interpretation of this portion of the Apocalypse to indicate a literal, physical reappearance of these Old Testament figures. The Gospels make it explicitly clear that St John the Baptist had fulfilled the prophecies of the coming of Elijah to prepare the way for the coming of the Messiah, not as a reincarnation or actual reappearance of this prophet from heaven, but rather that he came in the "spirit and power of Elijah" (*Lk* 1:17). It is through the ministry of the Two Witnesses that brings about the end-time conversion of the Jews, which as the *Catechism* states, must take place before the Second Coming of Christ:

> The glorious Messiah's coming is suspended at every moment of history until his recognition by "all Israel", for "a hardening has come upon part of Israel" in their

"unbelief" toward Jesus. St Peter says to the Jews of Jerusalem after Pentecost: "Repent therefore, and turn again, that your sins may be blotted out, that times of refreshing may come from the presence of the Lord, and that he may send the Christ appointed for you, Jesus, whom heaven must receive until the time for establishing all that God spoke by the mouth of his holy prophets from of old." St Paul echoes him: "For if their rejection means the reconciliation of the world, what will their acceptance mean but life from the dead?" The "full inclusion" of the Jews in the Messiah's salvation, in the wake of "the full number of the Gentiles", will enable the People of God to achieve "the measure of the stature of the fullness of Christ", in which "God may be all in all". (CCC 674)

It is here that we find the foundations for Pope St John Paul II's vision of a 'new springtime' for the Church, and his hopes for the success of the New Evangelisation.[34] The scriptural prophecies of the ministry of the Two Witnesses and the end-time conversion of the Jews are paralleled in private revelations by the promise of the conversion of nations such as Russia and England (e.g. in the secrets of Fatima and La Salette), and in the medieval prophecies of the reunification of the Eastern Orthodox and Catholic Churches under the auspices of the Angelic Pope. Taken together, these prophecies constitute a widespread expectation of a universal religious revival towards the end of the world, in a future period of Church history commonly known as the Second Pentecost.

The Millennium Strikes Back

Despite the warnings of Pope John Paul II not to distort the expectation of the renewal of the Church during the Second Pentecost into a 'new millenarianism', there has been a tendency in some quarters to reject the Augustinian tradition upheld by the Church, and equate the era of peace foretold in the second part of the Secret of Fatima with the millennium of Rv 20.[35] According to this view, the millennial reign of Christ did not begin with his ministry, death and resurrection, but is still to arrive in the future, during the 'era of peace', when evil will finally be defeated and Satan bound for a thousand years so that he can no longer tempt the elect. Those who hold to this system, exemplified by the writings of Fr Joseph Iannuzzi, attempt to avoid the charge of millenarianism by postulating that Christ will reign on earth invisibly in the Eucharist during this future millennial kingdom, as opposed to in the flesh.[36] Dr Paul Thigpen has dubbed this particular teaching as 'spiritual millenarianism'.[37] Those who hold this spiritual view of the millennium erroneously attempt to confine the meaning of the word 'millenarianism' to apply only to the doctrine of a physical reign of Christ on earth - a teaching which relates specifically to the central tenets of chiliasm.[38]

While it is true that the terms 'millenarian' and 'chiliasm' were interchangeable during the days of the early Church, the word 'millenarianism' has since taken on a very broad sense to include any group that teaches the imminent coming of a total transformation of society, in which the triumph over evil leads to the creation of an earthly utopia during a new dispensation for the world.[39] As such, there are also non-Christian forms of millenarianism, and Norman Cohn, one of the leading experts in this field, has even identified ideologies such as Marxism and Nazism as modern secular forms of millenarianism.[40] In fact, it is the secular form of millenarianism that is particularly singled out for condemnation by the *Catechism*:

> The Church has rejected even modified forms of this falsification of the kingdom to come under the name of millenarianism, especially the "intrinsically perverse" political form of a secular messianism. (CCC 676)

So we know that the *Catechism* is not solely condemning the doctrine of chiliasm here, but rather all forms of millenarianism, and especially the political type of secular messianism that was embodied by individuals such as Adolf Hitler, Vladimir Lenin, Joseph Stalin or Mao Zedong, which purported to be able to establish an earthly utopia through totalitarian means - usually by uniting the people against a perceived evil. The *Catechism* elucidates that the true nature of the error of millenarianism is in what political philosopher Eric Voegelin describes as "immanentising the eschaton" - the Promethean attempt to establish heaven here on earth without the need for God:

> The Antichrist's deception already begins to take shape in the world every time the claim is made to realise within history that messianic hope which can only be realised beyond history through the eschatological judgement. (CCC 676)

The real essence of what the *Catechism* is warning against here is the age-old temptation for humanity to deceive itself into thinking that it can be elevated to godhood here on earth - a temptation which is only further heightened through the insidious implications of an atheistic worldview. In doing so, we become guilty of the level of presumption condemned by St Paul, and in exchanging "the truth about God for a lie" we worship and serve "the creature rather than the Creator" (*Rm* 1:25). Envy of the absolute authority of God was the sin that caused Lucifer to fall from grace (*Is* 14:13-15), and the very first proposal that the Ancient Serpent put to humanity was that we could become like God ourselves (*Gn* 3:5). It is the atheistic mindset that causes the Most Holy Place to become desolate, enabling the man of lawlessness to take his seat in the Temple of God (*2 Th* 2:4). The ultimate goal of the lord of this world is to fill the vacancy left in the absence of God, and enthrone himself as god on this very earth, inviting us to participate in this rebellion. As the *Catechism* states: "The supreme religious deception is that of the Antichrist, a pseudo-messianism by which man glorifies himself in place of God and of his Messiah come in the flesh" (CCC 675).

The temptation that the Devil attempted to entice Jesus with in the desert was the promise of unlimited material power here on earth, if only he would make himself subject to Satan.

> And the devil took him up, and showed him all the kingdoms of the world in a moment of time, and said to him, "To you I will give all this authority and their glory; for it has been delivered to me, and I give it to whom I will. If you, then, will worship me, it shall all be yours." (*Lk* 4:5-7)

While Christ rejected any aspirations towards wielding earthly power outright, the Apocalypse tells us that this will be fully embraced by the Antichrist: "And to it the dragon gave his power and his throne and great authority" (*Rv* 13:2).

It is the distorted perception of the importance of the material world that allows the potential for a falsification of the kingdom to come, which the Magisterium vigorously condemns as the principal error of millenarianism and the deception of the Antichrist.

The Final Passover of the Church

As the *Catechism* teaches, the ultimate triumph of the Church is not destined to take place on earth within human history, but can only be achieved by taking up the Cross of Christ and following him in his death and resurrection:

> The Church will enter the glory of the kingdom only through this final Passover, when she will follow her Lord in his death and Resurrection. The kingdom will be fulfilled, then, not by a historic triumph of the Church through a progressive ascendancy, but only by God's victory over the final unleashing of evil, which will cause his Bride to come down from heaven. God's triumph over the revolt of evil will take the form of the Last Judgement after the final cosmic upheaval of this passing world. (CCC 677)

It is only through suffering the trial of a final Passover (which takes place during the Great Tribulation and persecution of the Antichrist) that the Church will finally enter the kingdom of God during the creation of the new heaven and new earth. This final Passover of the Church is reflected in last part of the Secret of Fatima, during which the shepherd children had a vision of a pope, together with the rest of the faithful, ascending their own personal Calvary:

And we saw in an immense light that is God: "something similar to how people appear in a mirror when they pass in front of it" a Bishop dressed in White "we had the impression that it was the Holy Father". Other Bishops, Priests, men and women Religious going up a steep mountain, at the top of which there was a big Cross of rough-hewn trunks as of a cork-tree with the bark; before reaching there the Holy Father passed through a big city half in ruins and half trembling with halting step, afflicted with pain and sorrow, he prayed for the souls of the corpses he met on his way; having reached the top of the mountain, on his knees at the foot of the big Cross he was killed by a group of soldiers who fired bullets and arrows at him, and in the same way there died one after another the other Bishops, Priests, men and women Religious, and various lay people of different ranks and positions. Beneath the two arms of the Cross there were two Angels each with a crystal aspersorium in his hand, in which they gathered up the blood of the Martyrs and with it sprinkled the souls that were making their way to God.

While the idea that an ultimate triumph over evil can be attained in this life may be comforting for some, the Gospels are consistently clear that the way of Christ is one of suffering, and that victory over the Devil can only be won by enduring the agony of the Cross.

"If any want to become my followers, let them deny themselves and take up their cross and follow me. For those who want to save their life will lose it, and those who lose their life for my sake will find it. For what will it profit them if they gain the whole world but forfeit their life?" (*Mt* 26:24-26)

By arguing that the era of peace promised by Our Lady of Fatima should be equated with the millennial reign of Christ described in *Rv* 20, contemporary spiritual millenarians not only contradict the Augustinian tradition which forms the basis of the eschatology outlined in the *Catechism*, but they also deny that the kingdom of God already exists on earth in the Church, and instead await the binding of Satan to take place in the future. In addition, they are confounded by some rather straightforward chronological details that can be gleaned from Scripture.

As we have already seen, the period of the new Pentecost is inaugurated by the ministry of the Two Witnesses, whose careers overlap that of the Antichrist. The Book of Revelation tells us that the Elijah who restores all things (*Mt* 17:11), who is identified with one of the Two Witnesses, will be put to death by the Antichrist as soon as his ministry is completed:

…when they have finished their testimony, the beast that ascends from the bottomless pit will make war upon them and conquer them and kill them, and their dead bodies will lie in the street of the great city which is allegorically called Sodom and Egypt, where their Lord was crucified. (*Rv* 11:7-8)

The implications here are clear. The period of the Second Pentecost, which brings in the fullness of the gentiles and the conversion of the Jews, must be of a relatively short duration that can be included within the scope of a normal human lifespan. As soon as the eternal Gospel has been preached to all nations, the Antichrist will then be revealed to the world and bring about the final persecution of the Church, which involves the martyrdom of the very people who are responsible for the restoration of the Church at the end time:

And this gospel of the kingdom will be preached throughout the whole world, as a testimony to all nations; and then the end will come. So when you see the desolating sacrilege spoken of by the prophet Daniel, standing in the holy place (let the reader understand), then let those who are in Judea flee to the mountains… (*Mt* 24:14-16)

Then I saw another angel flying in midheaven, with an eternal gospel to proclaim to those who dwell on earth, to every nation and tribe and tongue and people; and he said with a loud voice, "Fear God and give him glory, for the hour of his judgement has come…" (*Rv* 14:6-7)

The same sequence of events is also followed by authentic private revelations, wherein the Antichrist invariably appears immediately after the restoration of the Church by the Angelic Pope and the Great Monarch. For example, this order of chronology is closely adhered to by the original, Church approved 1851 version of the Secrets of La Salette:

> A great country, now Protestant, in the north of Europe, will be converted; by the support of this country all the other nations of the world will be converted. Before all that arrives, great disorders will arrive, in the Church, and everywhere. Then, after [that], our Holy Father the Pope will be persecuted. His successor will be a pontiff that nobody expects. Then, after [that], a great peace will come, but it will not last a long time. A monster will come to disturb it.

The Eschatological Harvest

Although he will subject the Church to its fiercest persecution in history, Scripture informs us that the revelation of the Antichrist will in turn be brought to nothing by the appearance of Christ during his Parousia. Just as the world was created through the utterance of the Divine Word, which became flesh as the Son of God, history will be brought to a close through the pronouncement of the Logos - which takes the shape of a sword issued from the mouth of Christ. Recalling the flaming sword which stands guard at the entrance to Eden to protect the way to the Tree of Life (*Gn* 3:24), it is this sword which brings about the destruction of the Antichrist. As the *Catechism* states:

> The Last Judgement will come when Christ returns in glory. Only the Father knows the day and the hour; only he determines the moment of its coming. Then through his Son Jesus Christ he will pronounce the final word on all history. (CCC 1040)

> And then the lawless one will be revealed, and the Lord Jesus will slay him with the breath of his mouth and destroy him by his appearing and his coming. (*2 Th* 2:8)

> From his mouth issues a sharp sword with which to smite the nations, and he will rule them with a rod of iron; he will tread the wine press of the fury of the wrath of God the Almighty. (*Rv* 19:15)

> And I saw the beast and the kings of the earth with their armies gathered to make war against him who sits upon the horse and against his army. And the beast was captured, and with it the false prophet who in its presence had worked the signs by which he deceived those who had received the mark of the beast and those who worshipped its image. These two were thrown alive into the lake of fire that burns with brimstone. And

the rest were slain by the sword of him who sits upon the horse, the sword that issues from his mouth; and all the birds were gorged with their flesh. (*Rv* 19:19-21)

During his Parousia, Christ does not come to establish a millennial reign of peace, but rather he brings the sword of judgement which sets the world on fire.

"Do not think that I have come to bring peace on earth; I have not come to bring peace, but a sword." (*Mt* 10:34)

"I came to cast fire upon the earth; and would that it were already kindled! I have a baptism to be baptised with; and how I am constrained until it is accomplished! Do you think that I have come to give peace on earth? No, I tell you, but rather division… (*Lk* 12:49-51)

…by the word of God heavens existed long ago, and an earth formed out of water and by means of water, through which the world that then existed was deluged with water and perished. But by the same word the heavens and earth that now exist have been stored up for fire, being kept until the day of judgement and destruction of ungodly men. (*2 P* 3:5-7)

As the *Catechism* teaches, the Second Coming of Christ is only delayed until the conversion of the Jews during the eschatological restoration of the Church, which brings in the fullness of the gentiles (CCC 674). Once the Bride has prepared herself for the wedding feast by adorning the pure white garments that will be granted to it during the eschatological outpouring of Holy Spirit, the Bridegroom will finally arrive to participate in the wedding feast of the Lamb (*Rv* 19:7-8). It is both the Holy Spirit and the Bride who summon the Groom to the banquet: "The Spirit and the Bride say, 'Come' (*Rv* 22:17). The pure garments worn by the Bride of the new Pentecost are made white in the blood of the Lamb during the final Passover of the Church:

> Then one of the elders addressed me, saying, "Who are these, clothed in white robes, and whence have they come?" I said to him, "Sir, you know." And he said to me, "These are they who have come out of the great tribulation; they have washed their robes and made them white in the blood of the Lamb". (*Rv* 7:13-14)

As Tertullian once famously said, "the blood of the martyrs is the seed of the Church". Just as a grain of wheat must die and fall to the ground to produce seed (*Jn* 12:24), the blood of the martyrs must be spilled during the great tribulation in order to bear fruit in the general resurrection of the dead. It is their blood crying from the ground for vengeance which compels Christ to execute his judgement upon the world (*Rv* 6:9-11).

The original Jewish celebration of Pentecost, the feast of *Shavuot* (the Festival of Weeks), marked the period of the first harvest, and was also known as the Festival of Reaping (*hag ha-Katsir*), or the Day of First Fruits (*yom ha-Bikkurim*). There appears to be a certain amount of symbolism here in connection with the appearance of Christ to reap the eschatological harvest at the end of time:

> Then I looked, and lo, a white cloud, and seated on the cloud one like a son of man, with a golden crown on his head, and a sharp sickle in his hand. And another angel came out of the temple, calling with a loud voice to him who sat upon the cloud, "Put in your sickle, and reap, for the hour to reap has come, for the harvest of the earth is fully ripe." So he who sat upon the cloud swung his sickle on the earth, and the earth was reaped. (*Rv* 14:14-16)

Given that *Shavout* also commemorates the day the Torah was given to the nation of Israel assembled at Mount Sinai, there is a further parallel here with the proclamation of the eternal Gospel to the entire world before the hour of judgement. Once the new Pentecost brings in both the fullness of the gentiles and the conversion of the Jews, the harvest will be fully ripe for the time of reaping, when both the wheat and the tares will be gathered together at the Last Judgement (*Mt* 13:24-30).

"…when the grain is ripe, at once he puts in the sickle, because the harvest has come" (*Mk* 4:29).

"I baptise you with water for repentance, but he who is coming after me is mightier than I, whose sandals I am not worthy to carry; he will baptise you with the Holy Spirit and with fire. His winnowing fork is in his hand, and he will clear his threshing floor and gather his wheat into the granary, but the chaff he will burn with unquenchable fire." (*Mt* 3:11-12)

It is then that the general resurrection of the dead will take place, when the elect will be gathered from the four corners of the earth to stand before the throne of God (*Mt* 24:31; *1 Th* 4:16-17; *Rv* 20:11-12). During the Great White Throne Judgement, the wicked are resurrected in the flesh alongside the just, including the Antichrist and the False Prophet, who then must face the consequences of their actions by being cast into the lake of eternal fire along with the Devil (*Rv* 19:20; 20:10). The chaos of the Apocalypse is then completely turned on its head, when the world is then restored to its original, pristine state during the new creation (*Rv* 21:1-4; *Is* 11:6-10). All things are then made new, and once the immortal soul of the first resurrection is again reunited with the physical body, the righteous enter into the eternal bliss of the beatific vision. It is only through following Christ in his Passover and resurrection that the Church triumphs over evil forever, and the kingdom inaugurated by the life and ministry of Jesus is fully realised. The whole of human history, and the entire fullness of the eschaton, finds its centre in the Cross of Our Lord, which has achieved victory over death itself.

Endnotes

[1] See *Catechism of the Catholic Church* para. 2816: "The Kingdom of God lies ahead of us. It is brought near in the Word incarnate, it is proclaimed throughout the whole Gospel, and it has come in Christ's death and Resurrection. The Kingdom of God has been coming since the Last Supper and, in the Eucharist, it is in our midst. The kingdom will come in glory when Christ hands it over to his Father". Cf. Congregation for the Doctrine of the Faith *Dominus Iesus* V:18: "The kingdom of God, in fact, has an eschatological dimension: it is a reality present in time, but its full realization will arrive only with the completion or fulfilment of history".

[2] *Catechism of the Catholic Church* para. 675

[3] See Joseph Card. Ratzinger, Theological Commentary, The Message of Fatima (2000). Cf. *Catechism of the Catholic Church*, paras 66-67

[4] St Irenaeus *Against Heresies* 5:32

[5] Ibid. 5:28

[6] Plato, *Timaeus* 39d

[7] Berossus *Babylonica*, cited in Seneca, *Naturales Quaestiones*, 3. 28 7-3. 29

[8] St Hippolytus, *Commentary on Daniel*, 2:4

[9] St Justin Martyr, *Dialouge with Trypho*, Chapter 80

[10] St Augustine, *City of God* Book XX, Chapter 7

[11] Ibid. Chapter 8

[12] Ibid.

[13] Ibid.

[14] Ibid. Chapter 12

[15] Ibid. Chapter 6

[16] In his treatise *Heroic Virtue: On the Beatification and Canonization of the Servants of God* (1750), Pope Benedict XIV states: "The recipients of prophecy may be angels, devils, men, women, children, heathens or gentiles; nor is it necessary that a man should be gifted with any particular disposition in order to receive the light of prophecy provided his intellect and senses be adapted for making manifest the things which God reveals to him. Though moral goodness is most profitable to a prophet, yet it is not necessary in order to obtain the gift of prophecy." (Vol 3, p. 149)

[17] St Thomas Aquinas, *Summa Theologica* SS 176

[18] Part of the original 1851 version of the secrets of La Salette, runs as follows: "A great king will go up on the throne, and will reign many years. Religion will re-flourish and spread all over the world, and there will be a great abundance. The world, glad to be lacking nothing, will fall again into disorder, will give up God, and will return to its criminal passions." First published in the 2002 book *Découverte du secret de La Salette* by Fr Michel Corteville and Fr Rene Laurentin, the 1851 versions of the secrets of La Salette retain full Church approval, while the later versions of Melanie's secret (which contained a substantial amount of additional material) was placed on the Index of Forbidden Books.

[19] Adso, Letter on the Origin and Life of the Antichrist, Trans. Bernard McGinn, *Visions of the End*, p. 86

[20] Tertullian, *On the Resurrection*, ch. 24

[21] Joachim de Fiore, *Exposition of the Apocalypse*

[22] Ibid. fol. 168ra. Cited in McGinn, B. *Antichrist: Two Thousand Years of Human Fascination with Evil*, p. 142

[23] It should be noted that the personal holiness of Joachim de Fiore is undisputed (which is reflected in the fact that he is still venerated as a beatus), and that since his theories were never condemned during his own lifetime, he cannot be considered to be a heretic. The Joachite movement however, stood by these views even after they had been condemned by the Church, and is thus considered heretical.

[24] Peter Olivi, *Commentary on Revelation*, cited in McGinn, B. *Visions of the End*, pp. 210-211

[25] First Vatican Council, Session IV, cap. 4

[26] Other examples of the spurious material circulated by such books include fantastical prophecies concerning the development of technology during the twentieth century, attributed to St Nilus of Sinai (d. 430), as well as Great Monarch prophecies attributed to figures such as St Caesarius of Arles (468-542) and St Cataldus of Taranto (d.685).

[27] St Hildegard of Bingen, *Scivias*, 3:11

[28] St Hildegard of Bingen, Letter to Werner von Kirchheim and his Priestly Community, PL 197, 269ff.

[29] Address of his Holiness Benedict XVI on the occasion of Christmas greetings to the Roman Curia, 10th December 2010

[30] St Hildegard of Bingen, *Scivias*, 3:11. Trans. McGinn, B. *Visions of the End*, p. 102

[31] See St Louis de Montfort, *Treatise on True Devotion*, paras 49-50

[32] Tarcisio Card. Bertone, *The Last Secret of Fatima*, pp. 10-11. It is noteworthy that Our Lady of All Nations, Amsterdam, 1945-1959 is omitted from Cardinal Bertone's list, which may indicate that the Congregation for the Doctrine of the Faith does not agree with Bishop Joseph Punt's approval, which was given in 2002. The approval of the miraculous events surrounding the statue of Our

Lady of Good Success in Quito, Ecuador, 1906, should be distinguished from the prophecies attributed to Mother Mariana de Jésus Torres of Quito (1563-1635) concerning the twentieth century, which contain more than a few anachronisms (such as the use of the terms 'masonry' and 'the Republic of Ecuador'). Our Lady of Knock (1879) is not listed here because the successive Archbishops of Tuam have never made any official pronouncement on this matter. However, the theological commissions appointed by Archbishop John MacHale in 1879 and Archbishop Thomas Gilmartin in 1936 both returned with a positive verdict. The Knock shrine was also conferred with the Golden Rose by Pope John Paul II in 1979, and it is the site of one of Ireland's only two basilicas.

[33] St Bonaventure, Collation 16:17-19. Translated by McGinn, B. *Visions of the End*, pp. 199-200

[34] See Pope John Paul II, *Redemptoris Missio*

[35] Pope John Paul II, *Tertio Millennio Adveniente* paras 18, 23

[36] See Iannuzzi, Joseph, *The Triumph of God's Kingdom in the Millennium and End Times: A Proper Belief From the Truth in Scripture and Church Teachings*, pp. 9-43

[37] Thigpen, Paùl, *The Rapture Trap*, pp. 204-205

[38] The teachings of Joachim de Fiore could similarly be described as 'spiritual millenarianism', given they do not hold to a physical reign of Christ during the millennium either, but rather a third dispensation presided over by the Holy Spirit. However, the Joachite movement is usually simply referred to as being millenarian in nature.

[39] See Cohn, N. *The Pursuit of the Millennium*, pp. 15-16

[40] Ibid. p. 109